¡Gracias tierra!
Thank you Earth!

MRS. SEÑORA

¡Gracias tierra!
Copyright © 2023 by Gilda Kupferman

All rights reserved. No part of this publication may be reproduced, distributed, or transmitted in any form or by any means, including photocopying, recording, or other electronic or mechanical methods, without the prior written permission of the author, except in the case of brief quotations embodied in critical reviews and certain other non-commercial uses permitted by copyright law.

Tellwell Talent
www.tellwell.ca

ISBN
978-0-2288-9427-8 (Hardcover)
978-0-2288-9426-1 (Paperback)

¡Gracias sol!
Thank you, sun!

¡Gracias luna!
Thank you, moon!

¡Gracias estrellas!
Thank you, stars!

¡Gracias agua!
Thank you, water!

¡Gracias aire!
Thank you, air!

¡Gracias tierra!
Thank you, Earth!

Mrs. Señora was born in Callao, Peru, and has lived in South Florida for over 40 years. For the past 20 years Mrs. Señora has taught Spanish in Fort Lauderdale, Florida. Mrs. Señora is a mother of three adorable bilingual children and she appreciates every moment with her family. The "Gracias" series was inspired by her grandmother, Mamá Mariana, who taught her to always be thankful.

¡Gracias Mamá Mariana!